# GERALD BARRY

## Piano Quartet No. 1

Music Department
OXFORD UNIVERSITY PRESS
Oxford and New York

Oxford University Press, Great Clarendon Street, Oxford OX2 6DP, England
Oxford University Press Inc., 198 Madison Avenue, New York, NY 10016, USA

Oxford is a trade mark of Oxford University Press

*Piano Quartet* was commissioned by the ICA with funds from London Arts.
It was first performed at the Institute of Contemporary Arts in London
on 6 December 1992 by Capricorn. It has been recorded on NMC D022
by Nua Nós, with Noriko Kawai, piano.


Accidentals apply only to the notes they precede.


INSTRUMENTATION
Piano
Violin
Viola
Cello


Performance material is available for sale or hire from the hire library.


Duration: 12 minutes

# Piano Quartet No. 1

GERALD BARRY
(1992)

Printed in Great Britain

OXFORD UNIVERSITY PRESS, MUSIC DEPARTMENT, GREAT CLARENDON STREET, OXFORD OX2 6DP

2

20

Solo: Hommage à Horowitz

♩ = 168

*fff* octaves played with complete abandon

* Viola and cello play these four quavers as triplet quavers with violin and piano.

\* Viola and cello omit last third of triplet, to align with violin and piano on first beat of next bar.

Printed by
Halstan & Co. Ltd., Amersham, Bucks., England

Music origination by
Barnes Music Engraving Ltd., East Sussex